Irresistible
Ice Pops

Sunil Vijayakar

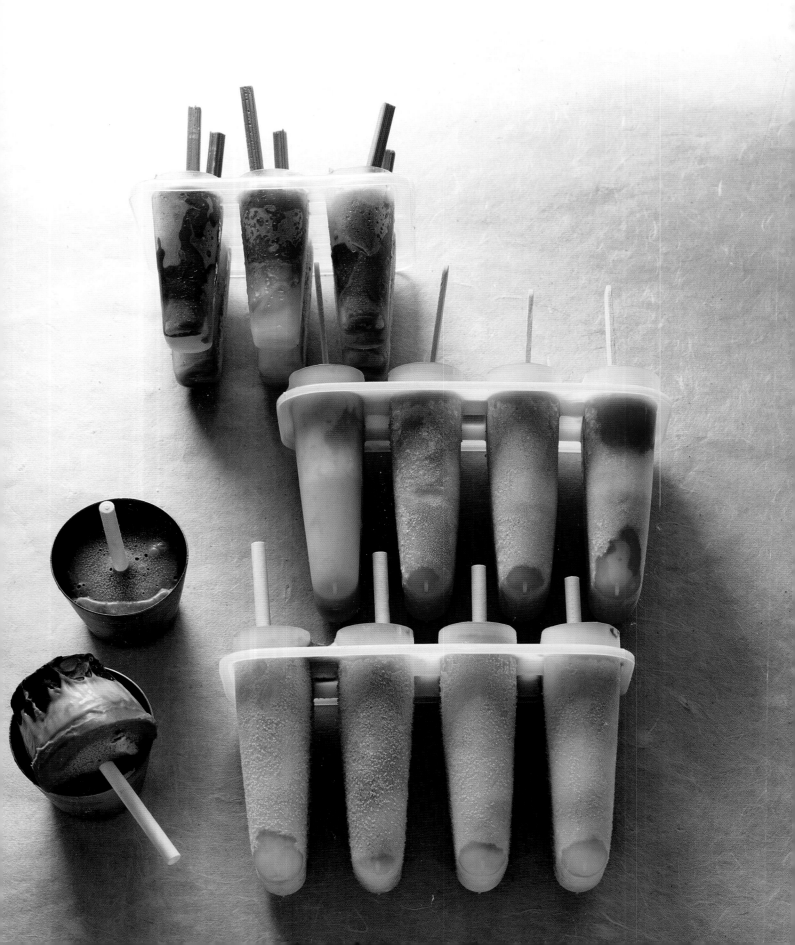

Irresistible Ice Pops

Sunil Vijayakar

First published in 2012

LOVE FOOD is an imprint of Parragon Books Ltd

Parragon
Queen Street House
4 Queen Street
Bath BA1 1HE, UK

www.parragon.com

ISBN: 978-1-4454-7775-6

Printed in China

Created and produced by Pene Parker and Becca Spry
Author and home economist: Sunil Vijayakar
Photographer: Karen Thomas

Notes for the Reader

This book uses both metric and imperial measurements. Follow the same units of measurements throughout;
do not mix metric and imperial. All spoon measurements are level: teaspoons are assumed to be 5 ml,
and tablespoons are assumed to be 15 ml. Unless otherwise stated, milk is assumed to be full fat and eggs
and individual fruits are medium.

The times given are an approximate guide only. Preparation times differ according to the techniques used by
different people and the cooking times may also vary from those given. Optional ingredients, variations or serving
suggestions have not been included in the calculations.

Pregnant and breastfeeding women are advised to avoid eating peanuts and peanut products. Sufferers from nut
allergies should be aware that some of the ready-made ingredients used in the recipes in this book may contain nuts.
Always check the packaging before use.

Contents

Introduction 6

Fresh and Fruity 10

Indulgent 28

New and Zingy 46

Pops with a Kick 62

Index 80

Making Your Own Ice Pops

It all started in San Francisco in 1905, when an 11-year-old boy, Frank Epperson, accidentally left a mixture of sweetened soda water in a cup, with a stirring stick, out on his porch. It was a freezing night and Frank awoke the next morning to discover a frozen 'ice pop'.

The rest is history, and now ice pops come in all shapes, flavours, colours and sizes. The simplest ones are fruit juice-based, and the more elaborate ones have many layers of flavour and colour.

You and your children can make wonderful ice pops with different flavours, textures and shapes with the minimum of equipment. It's a great way to get kids involved in cooking and excited about creating their own flavours.

Sugar Syrup

You can make ice pops from almost any fruit or flavouring, but there are some things you should consider when it comes to freezing them. The secret to making most ice pops soft and smooth is the inclusion of a sugar syrup. This lowers the freezing point of a liquid and acts as a lubricant between the ice crystals. Dissolving or mixing it into the base ingredients will allow the flavours to be distributed evenly and create a smooth and delicious treat. Here is the recipe for sugar syrup, which is easy to make.

Makes: 250 ml/9 fl oz
Prep: 5 minutes
Cook: 8–10 minutes
Cool: 1 hour

* 90 g/3¼ oz caster sugar
* 200 ml/7 fl oz water

1. Put the sugar and water in a small saucepan. Cook over a low heat, stirring, for 6–8 minutes or until all the sugar has dissolved.

2. Increase the heat to high until the mixture comes to the boil, then reduce the heat to medium and simmer for 3–4 minutes.

3. Remove from the heat, cover and allow to cool completely.

4. Store the cooled syrup in a sealed container in the refrigerator for up to a week.

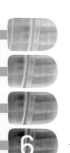

Equipment

Ice pops are so easy to make that you will require very little equipment. Apart from ice pop moulds and sticks, the most important thing you'll need is a blender, which you can use to purée fruit mixtures for the recipes. If you want a silky smooth texture to your puréed fruit, you will also need a metal sieve to scrape the mixture through before discarding the pips and seeds. And, of course, you need a freezer!

Ice Pop Moulds

You can get an amazing variety of ice pop moulds on-line, in supermarkets and in good kitchen shops. They come in various shapes and sizes. However, you don't have to buy special moulds; instead, be creative and use other freezable containers such as metal ramekins, individual pudding basins, tartlet tins, small paper cups, recycled yogurt pots or any short or narrow glass. The only thing to keep in mind is that the top of a mould should be wider than, or the same diameter as, the rest of it, so the ice pops can be unmoulded easily.

Ice Pop Sticks

Most shop-bought ice pop moulds come with a built-in lolly stick. You can also buy wooden lolly sticks from craft stores or on-line. Buy them in bulk, as they are inexpensive and great for having to hand for spontaneous ice pop making. If you don't have ice pop sticks, you can substitute things like long cinnamon sticks and lemon grass stalks for an unusual twist.

Techniques and Tips

Inserting Ice Pop Sticks

If you are using shop-bought moulds with their own plastic sticks, follow the manufacturer's instructions on inserting the sticks. If your moulds don't come with sticks, use wooden ones. You will need a way to hold the sticks in place while your ice pop freezes. The easiest and most effective way is to cover the filled moulds with foil and make a small slit with a sharp knife in the centre. Insert the stick and it will be secure until your ice pop is frozen. If the ice pop mixture is quite liquid, you might have to freeze the mixture for about an hour, or until it is slushy, before you insert the stick and continue to freeze until solid.

Filling Ice Pop Moulds

During freezing, the ingredients will expand, so care must be taken when filling the moulds to leave at least a 5–15 mm/¼–⅝ inch space at the top. Also keep in mind that some liquid mixtures, such as cola, sodas and lemonade, have a high air content and will expand more than denser mixtures such as puréed fruit, yogurt and cream.

Alcohol in Ice Pops

Since alcohol freezes at a much lower temperature than water, don't use too much of it in your ice pop mixture or it will not freeze well. Pops containing alcohol are shown by this symbol and should only be eaten by adults.

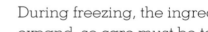

Unmoulding Ice Pops

There are two ways of unmoulding an ice pop: you can dip the frozen moulds into warm water for a few seconds and gently release the pops while holding on to the sticks; alternatively, you can wrap the mould in a hot water-soaked tea-towel until the pop can be unmoulded.

'Do not restrict yourself to the recipes in this book… adapt them to suit your tastes and freeze up some fun in the kitchen!'

Fresh and Fruity

Strawberry Sensations   12

Blueberry and Pink Lemonade Lollies   14

Summer Melon Medley Pops   16

Fruit Cocktail Pops   18

Raspberry and Banana Layer Pops   20

Very Cherry Ripple Pops   22

Pomegranate Power Pops   24

Blackberry and Orange Bursts   26

Strawberry Sensations

Makes: 8 ice pops

Prep: 10 minutes

Freeze: 6–8 hours

Eat: within 3 months of freezing

Kids will go mad for these wild, colourful and tasty iced treats – especially if you use fun moulds such as rockets!

* 400 ml/14 fl oz cranberry juice
* 1 tsp finely grated orange rind
* 250 ml/9 fl oz sugar syrup (see page 6)
* 6 large strawberries, hulled and cut into thin slices

1. Put the cranberry juice, orange rind and sugar syrup into a measuring jug and stir together well.

2. Pour half the cranberry mixture into 8 x 100 ml/3½ fl oz ice pop moulds. (Put the rest of the mixture in the refrigerator, covered.)

3. Drop half the strawberry slices into the moulds, ensuring you have an even number of slices in each one. (Put the rest of the slices in the refrigerator, covered.) Insert the ice pop sticks (see page 8) and freeze for 3–4 hours, or until firm.

4. Pour the remaining cranberry mixture into the moulds, then drop in the remaining strawberry slices. Freeze for 3–4 hours, or until firm.

5. To unmould the ice pops, dip the frozen moulds into warm water for a few seconds and gently release the pops while holding the sticks.

Blueberry and Pink Lemonade Lollies

Makes: 8 ice pops

Prep: 10 minutes

Freeze: 4–5 hours

Eat: within 3 months of freezing

Make these pretty, fruit-filled iced treats for a hot summer's day. Experiment by making them with other berries for more ice pop fun.

* 500 ml/18 fl oz pink lemonade, chilled
* juice of ½ lemon
* 100 ml/3½ fl oz sugar syrup (see page 6)
* 150 g/5½ oz blueberries

1. Put the pink lemonade, lemon juice and sugar syrup into a measuring jug and stir together well.

2. Drop the blueberries into 8 x 100 ml/3½ fl oz ice pop moulds, ensuring you have an even number of berries in each one.

3. Pour the lemonade mixture over the berries. Insert the ice pop sticks (see page 8) and freeze for 4–5 hours, or until firm.

4. To unmould the lollies, dip the frozen moulds into warm water for a few seconds and gently release the lollies while holding the sticks.

Summer Melon Medley Pops

Makes: 8 ice pops

Prep: 10 minutes

Freeze: 8 hours

Eat: within 3 months of freezing

Refreshing, cooling and full of fresh flavours, these melon ice pops will put a smile on anyone's face on a hot summer's day.

* juice and finely grated rind of 1 lime
* 100 ml/3½ fl oz sugar syrup (see page 6)
* 175 g/6 oz deseeded and roughly chopped watermelon flesh
* 175 g/6 oz deseeded and roughly chopped cantaloupe melon flesh

1. Put the lime juice, lime rind and sugar syrup into a measuring jug and stir together well.

2. Put the watermelon and half the lime syrup in a blender and whizz until smooth. Pour the mixture into 8 x 100 ml/3½ fl oz ice pop moulds. Freeze for 4 hours, or until firm.

3. When the watermelon mixture is frozen, put the cantaloupe melon and the remaining lime syrup in the blender and whizz until smooth. Pour over the frozen watermelon mixture. Insert the ice pop sticks (see page 8) and freeze for 4 hours, or until firm.

4. To unmould the ice pops, dip the frozen moulds into warm water for a few seconds and gently release the pops while holding the sticks.

Fruit Cocktail Pops

Makes: 8 ice pops

Prep: 15 minutes

Freeze: 6 hours

Eat: within 3 months of freezing

This is a wonderful way to capture the essence of summer, with the flavours and vibrant colours of ripe, juicy peaches, strawberries and kiwis.

* 200 g/7 oz strawberries, hulled
* 85 ml/3 fl oz sugar syrup (see page 6)
* 225 g/8 oz ripe peaches, peeled, stoned and roughly chopped (or 200 g/7 oz canned peaches)
* 4 large kiwi fruit, peeled and roughly chopped

1. Put the strawberries in a blender and whizz until puréed. Stir in a third of the sugar syrup. Pour the mixture into 8 x 100 ml/3½ fl oz ice pop moulds. Freeze for 2 hours, or until firm.

2. When the strawberry mixture is frozen, put the peaches in the blender and whizz until puréed. Stir in half of the remaining sugar syrup. Pour over the frozen strawberry mixture. Insert the ice pop sticks (see page 8) and freeze for 2 hours, or until firm.

3. When the peach mixture is frozen, put the kiwi fruit in the blender and whizz until puréed. Stir in the remaining sugar syrup. Pour over the frozen peach mixture and freeze for 2 hours, or until firm.

4. To unmould the ice pops, dip the frozen moulds into warm water for a few seconds and gently release the pops while holding the sticks.

Raspberry and Banana Layer Pops

Makes: 8 ice pops

Prep: 15 minutes

Freeze: 7–8 hours

Eat: within 3 months of freezing

Creamy vanilla yogurt is puréed with bananas and honey, then layered with a zingy raspberry purée, to create a beautiful and delicious ice pop.

* 3 ripe bananas
* 100 ml/3½ fl oz vanilla yogurt
* 8 tbsp runny honey
* 200 g/7 oz raspberries

1. Peel the bananas. Put them in a blender with the yogurt and half the honey and whizz until smooth.

2. Pour half of the banana mixture into 8 x 100 ml/3½ fl oz ice pop moulds. (Put the rest of the mixture in the refrigerator, covered.) Freeze for 2 hours, or until firm.

3. When the banana mixture is frozen, put the raspberries and remaining honey in the blender and whizz until puréed. Sieve out the seeds using a fine metal sieve. Pour over the frozen banana mixture. Insert the ice pop sticks (see page 8) and freeze for 2 hours, or until firm.

4. Pour the remaining banana mixture over the frozen raspberry mixture. Freeze for 3–4 hours, or until firm.

5. To unmould the ice pops, dip the frozen moulds into warm water for a few seconds and gently release the pops while holding the sticks.

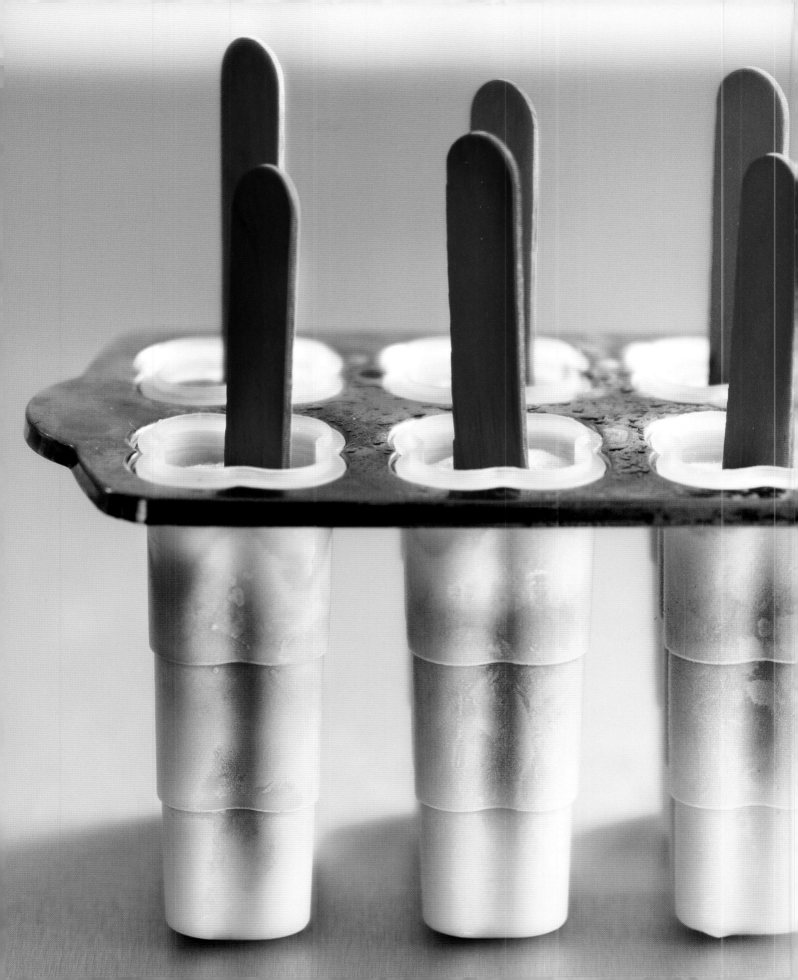

Very Cherry Ripple Pops

Makes: 8 ice pops

Prep: 20 minutes

Cool: 1 hour

Freeze: 4–5 hours

Eat: within 3 months of freezing

Heating the blackcurrants with the sugar and lemon rind intensifies their flavour and works really well with the rich cherry mixture.

* 200 g/7 oz blackcurrants
* 50 g/1¾ oz caster sugar
* finely grated rind of ½ lemon
* 75 ml/2½ fl oz water
* 100 ml/3½ fl oz cherry jam
* 200 ml/7 fl oz cherry yogurt

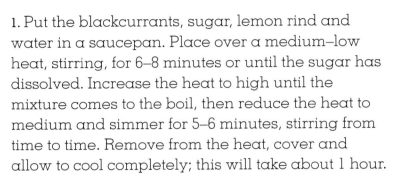

1. Put the blackcurrants, sugar, lemon rind and water in a saucepan. Place over a medium–low heat, stirring, for 6–8 minutes or until the sugar has dissolved. Increase the heat to high until the mixture comes to the boil, then reduce the heat to medium and simmer for 5–6 minutes, stirring from time to time. Remove from the heat, cover and allow to cool completely; this will take about 1 hour.

2. Whizz the mixture until smooth using a hand-held electric blender. Transfer to a wide bowl.

3. Put the cherry jam and yogurt in a separate bowl and, using a metal spoon, beat together until smooth. Gently swirl this mixture into the blackcurrant purée, folding through with a skewer to create a marbled effect.

4. Spoon the mixture into 8 x 100 ml/3½ fl oz ice pop moulds. Insert the ice pop sticks (see page 8) and freeze for 4–5 hours, or until firm.

5. To unmould the ice pops, dip the frozen moulds into warm water for a few seconds and gently release the pops while holding the sticks.

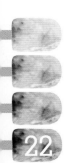

Pomegranate Power Pops

Makes: 8 ice pops
Prep: 15 minutes
Freeze: 9–10 hours
Eat: within 3 months
of freezing

You can buy pomegranate juice for this recipe, but you could also juice fresh pomegranates if you prefer. Simply cut them in half and squeeze the juice through a sieve into a bowl.

* 200 ml/7 fl oz pomegranate juice
* 200 ml/7 fl oz grapefruit juice
* 250 ml/9 fl oz sugar syrup
  (see page 6)
* 85 g/3 oz pomegranate seeds

1. Put the pomegranate juice and grapefruit juice into separate measuring jugs. Pour half the sugar syrup into each jug and stir together well.

2. Pour half the pomegranate mixture into 8 x 100 ml/3½ fl oz ice pop moulds. (Put the rest of the mixture and the grapefruit mixture in the refrigerator, covered.) Freeze for 2 hours, or until firm.

3. Pour half the grapefruit mixture over the frozen pomegranate mixture and drop in half the pomegranate seeds. (Put the rest of the mixture and seeds in the refrigerator, covered.) Insert the ice pop sticks (see page 8) and freeze for 2 hours, or until firm.

4. Pour the remaining pomegranate mixture over the frozen grapefruit mixture and freeze for 2 hours, or until firm.

5. Pour the remaining grapefruit mixture over the frozen pomegranate mixture and drop in the remaining pomegranate seeds. Freeze for 3–4 hours, or until firm.

6. To unmould the ice pops, dip the frozen moulds into warm water for a few seconds and gently release the pops while holding the sticks.

Blackberry and Orange Bursts

Makes: 8 ice pops

Prep: 10 minutes

Freeze: 4–5 hours

Eat: within 3 months of freezing

The combination of sweet blackberries, a rich citrus hit and the deep colour of blood orange juice will make these a guaranteed favourite with everyone.

* 500 ml/18 fl oz blood orange juice
* 100 ml/3½ fl oz sugar syrup (see page 6)
* 300 g/10½ oz blackberries

1. Put the blood orange juice and sugar syrup into a measuring jug and stir together well.

2. Drop the blackberries into 8 x 100 ml/3½ fl oz ice pop moulds, ensuring you have an even number of berries in each one.

3. Pour the blood orange juice mixture over the berries. Insert the ice pop sticks (see page 8) and freeze for 4–5 hours, or until firm.

4. To unmould the ice pops, dip the frozen moulds into warm water for a few seconds and gently release the pops while holding the sticks.

Indulgent

Peaches and Cream Pops   30

Choc Berry Rockets   32

Mango Fruity Crush Lollies   34

Chocolate Mint Delights   36

Yogurt Raspberry Ripple Pops   38

Triple Chocolate Heaven Pops   40

Banana Split Lollies   42

Dark Chocolate Ripple Pops   44

Peaches and Cream Pops

Makes: 8 ice pops

Prep: 15 minutes

Freeze: 6–7 hours

Eat: within 3 months of freezing

Peaches have to be fully ripe and heavy with juice to be enjoyed properly. This is a luxurious iced treat that will delight kids and grown-ups alike.

* 150 ml/5 fl oz single cream, lightly whipped
* 2 tbsp icing sugar
* 1 tsp vanilla extract
* 550 g/1 lb 4 oz ripe peaches, peeled, stoned and roughly chopped (or 500 g/1 lb 2 oz canned peaches)
* 100 ml/3½ fl oz sugar syrup (see page 6)

1. Put the cream, sugar and vanilla extract into a measuring jug and stir together well.

2. Pour the mixture into 8 x 100 ml/3½ fl oz ice pop moulds. Freeze for 2 hours, or until firm.

3. When the cream mixture is frozen, put the peaches and sugar syrup in a blender and whizz until puréed.

4. Pour the peach mixture over the frozen cream mixture. Insert the ice pop sticks (see page 8) and freeze for 4–5 hours, or until firm.

5. To unmould the ice pops, dip the frozen moulds into warm water for a few seconds and gently release the pops while holding the sticks.

Choc Berry Rockets

Makes: 8 ice pops

Prep: 25 minutes

Freeze: 4 hours
10 minutes–6 hours
20 minutes

Eat: within 3 months
of freezing

Kids can have fun making these tasty iced treats by dipping them into chocolate and edible sprinkles to create their very own masterpieces.

* 400 g/14 oz raspberries
* 2 tbsp lemon juice
* 250 ml/9 fl oz sugar syrup (see page 6)
* 250 g/9 oz plain chocolate, roughly chopped
* 100 g/3½ oz hundreds and thousands

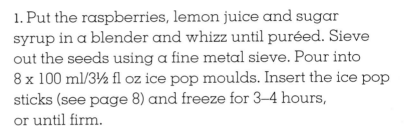

1. Put the raspberries, lemon juice and sugar syrup in a blender and whizz until puréed. Sieve out the seeds using a fine metal sieve. Pour into 8 x 100 ml/3½ fl oz ice pop moulds. Insert the ice pop sticks (see page 8) and freeze for 3–4 hours, or until firm.

2. When the raspberry mixture is frozen, line a baking sheet with baking paper. To unmould the ice pops, dip the frozen moulds into warm water for a few seconds and gently release the pops while holding the sticks. Place them on the prepared baking sheet and return to the freezer for 1–2 hours.

3. When the ice pops are frozen, put the chocolate in a heatproof bowl, set the bowl over a saucepan of gently simmering water and heat until melted. Remove from the heat and allow to cool slightly.

4. Tip the hundreds and thousands onto baking paper. Dip each ice pop into the melted chocolate so it is covered to about half-way up, then roll it in the hundreds and thousands. Return to the prepared baking sheet and freeze for 10–20 minutes, or until ready to serve.

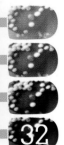

Mango Fruity Crush Lollies

Makes: 8 ice pops

Prep: 20 minutes

Freeze: 6–8 hours

Eat: within 3 months of freezing

These three-layered fruity and creamy treats are packed with colour, texture and flavour. The mango and strawberries work hand-in-hand with the vanilla.

* 300 ml/10½ fl oz mango purée
* 9 tbsp runny honey
* 300 ml/10½ fl oz vanilla yogurt
* 2 tsp vanilla extract
* 300 g/10½ oz strawberries, hulled

1. Put the mango purée and 3 tablespoons of the honey into a measuring jug and stir together well.

2. Pour the mixture into 8 x 100 ml/3½ fl oz ice pop moulds. Freeze for 2 hours, or until firm.

3. When the mango mixture is frozen, put the yogurt, vanilla extract and a further 3 tablespoons of the honey in a bowl and stir together well. Spoon over the frozen mango mixture. Insert the ice pop sticks (see page 8) and freeze for 2–3 hours, or until firm.

4. When the vanilla mixture is frozen, put the strawberries and remaining honey in a blender and whizz until puréed. Sieve out the seeds using a fine metal sieve. Pour over the frozen vanilla mixture and freeze for 2–3 hours, or until firm

5. To unmould the lollies, dip the frozen moulds into warm water for a few seconds and gently release the lollies while holding the sticks.

Chocolate Mint Delights

Makes: 8 ice pops

Prep: 25 minutes

Cool: 1 hour

Freeze: 6–8 hours

Eat: within 3 months of freezing

For a kid-friendly version of this chocolate-dipped minty pop, simply omit the crème de menthe and use milk chocolate instead of plain.

* 2 tbsp crème de menthe
* 250 ml/9 fl oz sugar syrup (see page 6)
* 500 ml/18 fl oz water
* a small handful of little fresh mint leaves
* 2–3 drops of green food colouring
* 200 g/7 oz plain chocolate, roughly chopped

1. Put the crème de menthe, sugar syrup and water in a saucepan. Place over a medium–high heat until the mixture comes to the boil, stirring. Remove from the heat, cover and allow to cool completely; this will take about 1 hour.

2. Stir in the mint leaves and green food colouring and pour into 8 x 80 ml/2½ fl oz ice pop moulds. Insert the ice pop sticks (see page 8) and freeze for 4 hours, or until firm.

3. When the mint mixture is frozen, line a baking sheet with baking paper. To unmould the ice pops, dip the frozen moulds into warm water for a few seconds and gently release the pops while holding the sticks. Place them on the prepared baking sheet and return to the freezer for 1–2 hours.

4. When the ice pops are frozen, put the chocolate in a heatproof bowl, set the bowl over a saucepan of gently simmering water and heat until melted. Remove from the heat and allow to cool slightly.

5. Dip each ice pop into the melted chocolate so it is covered to a third of the way up. Return to the prepared baking sheet and freeze for 1–2 hours, or until firm.

Yogurt Raspberry Ripple Pops

Makes: 8 ice pops

Prep: 20 minutes

Freeze: 4–5 hours

Eat: within 3 months of freezing

The classic combination of raspberries and cream is a guaranteed favourite, and this healthy version, using vanilla yogurt, makes a delicious frozen treat.

* 200 g/7 oz raspberries
* 100 ml/3½ fl oz sugar syrup (see page 6)
* 500 ml/18 fl oz vanilla yogurt
* 2 tsp vanilla extract

1. Put the raspberries and sugar syrup in a blender and whizz until smooth. Sieve out the seeds using a fine metal sieve. Transfer to a bowl.

2. Put the yogurt and vanilla extract in a bowl and stir together well. Gently swirl this mixture into the raspberry mixture, folding through with a skewer to create a marbled effect.

3. Spoon the mixture into 8 x 100 ml/3½ fl oz ice pop moulds. Insert the ice pop sticks (see page 8) and freeze for 4–5 hours, or until firm.

4. To unmould the ice pops, dip the frozen moulds into warm water for a few seconds and gently release the pops while holding the sticks.

Triple Chocolate Heaven Pops

Makes: 8 ice pops
Prep: 15 minutes
Cool: 10–12 minutes
Freeze: 3–4 hours
Eat: within 3 months
of freezing

For ultimate indulgence, these ice pops will surely hit all the right buttons with their creamy taste and triple chocolate hit.

* 300 ml/10 fl oz double cream
* 100 g/3½ oz plain chocolate, roughly chopped
* 100 g/3½ oz white chocolate, roughly chopped
* 100 g/3½ oz milk chocolate, roughly chopped

1. Divide the cream equally between 3 small saucepans. Put the plain chocolate in 1 of the pans, the white chocolate in another pan and the milk chocolate in the final pan.

2. Place each pan over a gentle heat and stir until the chocolate has melted and the mixture is smooth. Remove from the heat and allow to cool for 10–12 minutes.

3. Pour the dark chocolate mixture into 8 x 50 ml/1¾ fl oz ice pop moulds. Carefully pour the white chocolate mixture over the dark chocolate, then pour the milk chocolate mixture over the white chocolate. Insert the ice pop sticks (see page 8) and freeze for 3–4 hours, or until firm.

4. To unmould the ice pops, dip the frozen moulds into warm water for a few seconds and gently release the pops while holding the sticks.

Banana Split Lollies

Makes: 8 ice pops

Prep: 25 minutes

Freeze: 5 hours
10 minutes–6 hours
20 minutes

Eat: within 3 months
of freezing

The delicious chocolate and coconut coating on these ice pops complements the rich, creamy banana mixture that lies within.

* 4 bananas
* 6 tbsp icing sugar
* 2 tbsp coconut cream
* 100 ml/3½ fl oz vanilla yogurt
* 400 g/14 oz plain chocolate, roughly chopped
* 100 g/3½ oz sweetened desiccated coconut, to decorate

1. Peel the bananas. Put them in a blender with the icing sugar, coconut cream and yogurt and whizz until smooth. Pour the mixture into 8 x 60 ml/2¼ fl oz ice pop moulds. Insert the ice pop sticks (see page 8) and freeze for 4 hours, or until firm.

2. When the banana mixture is frozen, line a baking sheet with baking paper. To unmould the ice pops, dip the frozen moulds into warm water for a few seconds and gently release the pops while holding the sticks. Place them on the prepared baking sheet and return to the freezer for 1–2 hours.

3. Put the chocolate in a heatproof bowl, set the bowl over a saucepan of gently simmering water and heat until melted. Remove from the heat and allow to cool slightly.

4. Dip each ice pop into the melted chocolate, then sprinkle over the desiccated coconut. Return to the prepared baking sheet and freeze for 10–20 minutes, or until ready to serve.

Dark Chocolate Ripple Pops

Makes: 8 ice pops
Prep: 20 minutes
Freeze: 4–5 hours
Eat: within 3 months
of freezing

Chocolate and cream make a classic combination that brings these rippled pops to life, making you want more and more.

* 200 g/7 oz plain chocolate, roughly chopped
* 500 ml/18 fl oz double cream
* 100 ml/3½ fl oz sugar syrup (see page 6)

1. Put the chocolate and 100 ml/3½ fl oz of the cream in a small saucepan. Place over a medium–low heat, stirring, until melted and smooth. Remove from the heat and set aside to cool.

2. Meanwhile, pour the remaining cream into a wide bowl and lightly beat with an electric whisk until soft peaks form. Whisk in the sugar syrup.

3. Drizzle the melted chocolate mixture over the cream and fold through using a fork to create a rippled effect.

4. Carefully spoon the mixture into 8 x 80 ml/2½ fl oz ice pop moulds. Insert the ice pop sticks (see page 8) and freeze for 4–5 hours, or until firm.

5. To unmould the ice pops, dip the frozen moulds into warm water for a few seconds and gently release the pops while holding the sticks.

New and Zingy

Honeydew Heaven Pops   48

Lime and Chilli Sorbet Lollies   50

Watermelon Chill-out Lollies   52

Spiced Plum Pops   54

Coconut Passion Pops   56

Milky Chai Pops   58

Cappuccino Pops   60

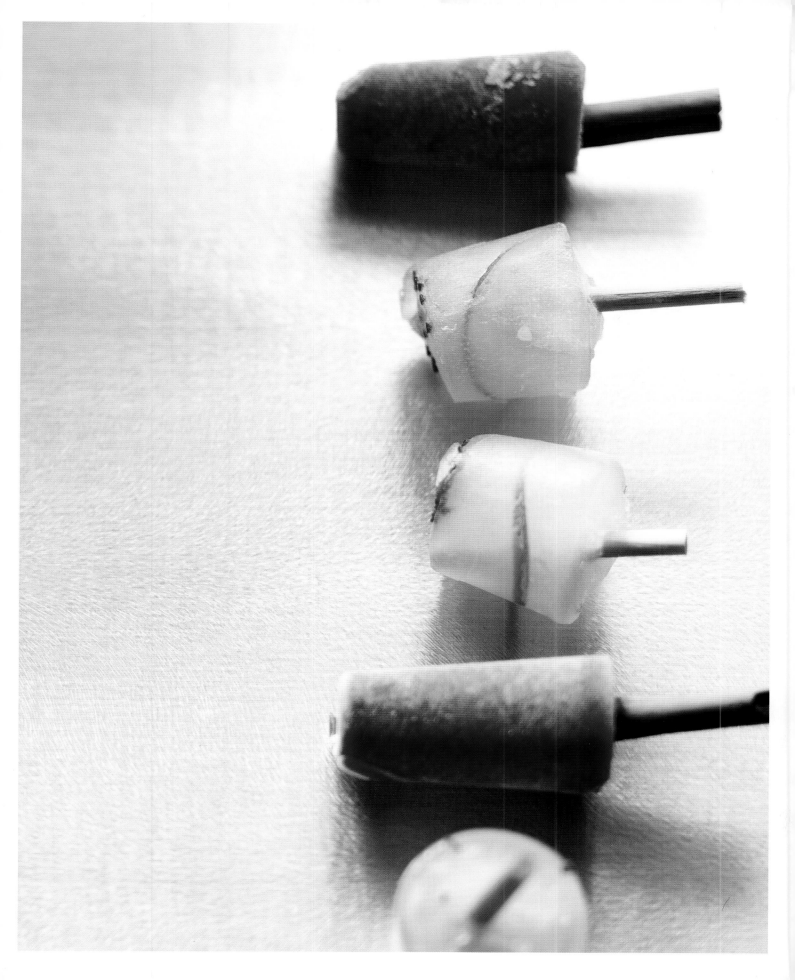

Honeydew Heaven Pops

Makes: 8 ice-pops

Prep: 15 minutes

Freeze: 4–5 hours

Eat: within 3 months of freezing

A gorgeously light ice pop; cooling on a hot afternoon and delicious as a dessert after a Thai or Indian meal.

* 600 g/1 lb 5 oz deseeded and roughly chopped honeydew melon flesh
* 8 tbsp runny honey
* 1 tbsp lemon grass paste or 1 tbsp very finely chopped lemon grass
* 100 ml/3½ fl oz fresh lemonade
* 8 lemon grass stalks

1. Put the melon, honey and lemon grass paste in a blender and whizz until puréed. Add the lemonade and whizz until smooth.

2. Pour the mixture into 8 x 100 ml/3½ fl oz ice pop moulds. Insert the lemon grass stalks as sticks (see page 8) and freeze for 4–5 hours, or until firm.

3. To unmould the ice pops, dip the frozen moulds into warm water for a few seconds and gently release the pops while holding the lemon grass stalks.

Lime and Chilli Sorbet Lollies

Makes: 8 ice pops
Prep: 15 minutes
Cool: 1 hour
Freeze: 5–6 hours
Eat: within 3 months
of freezing

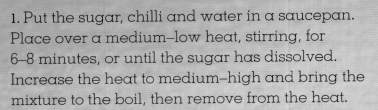

These pale, chilli-speckled sorbet sticks are a twist on the classic lemon sorbet, but have a hidden kick from the chilli. For a less spicy version, reduce the amount of chilli.

* 100 g/3½ oz caster sugar
* 1 red chilli, deseeded and very finely chopped
* 400 ml/14 fl oz water
* 4 large limes
* 8 very thin slices from a small lime

1. Put the sugar, chilli and water in a saucepan. Place over a medium–low heat, stirring, for 6–8 minutes, or until the sugar has dissolved. Increase the heat to medium–high and bring the mixture to the boil, then remove from the heat.

2. Finely grate the rind of 2 of the limes into the mixture and stir. Cover and allow to cool completely; this will take about 1 hour.

3. Squeeze the juice from the 4 limes and stir it into the mixture.

4. Pour the mixture into 8 x 60 ml/2¼ fl oz ice pop moulds and place a lime slice into each mould. Insert the ice-pop sticks (see page 8) and freeze for 5–6 hours, or until firm.

5. To unmould the ice pops, dip the frozen moulds into warm water for a few seconds and gently release the pops while holding the sticks.

Watermelon Chill-out Lollies

Makes: 8 ice pops

Prep: 10 minutes

Freeze: 6 hours

Eat: within 3 months
of freezing

A combination of basil and watermelon works brilliantly when brought together in this colourful iced treat.

* 500 g/1 lb 2 oz deseeded and roughly chopped watermelon flesh
* 100 ml/3½ fl oz sugar syrup (see page 6)
* 1 tbsp very finely chopped fresh basil leaves
* finely grated rind of 1 lime
* 16 small–medium fresh basil leaves

1. Put the watermelon, sugar syrup, chopped basil and lime rind in a blender and whizz until puréed and flecked.

2. Put 2 basil leaves into each of 8 x 80 ml/2½ fl oz ice pop moulds. Pour the watermelon mixture into the moulds. Insert the ice pop sticks (see page 8) and freeze for 6 hours, or until firm.

3. To unmould the ice pops, dip the frozen moulds into warm water for a few seconds and gently release the pops while holding the sticks.

Spiced Plum Pops

Makes: 8 ice pops

Prep: 15 minutes

Cool: 30 minutes

Freeze: 5 hours

Eat: within 3 months of freezing

This plum and spice mixture is bursting with late summer flavours, but with warming spice in the background.

* 400 g/14 oz ripe plums, peeled, halved, stoned and sliced
* 1 tsp ground cinnamon
* a pinch of ground cloves
* a pinch of ground star anise
* 75 g/2¾ oz caster sugar
* 100 ml/3½ fl oz water
* juice of 1 orange
* 8 cinnamon sticks

1. Put the plums, cinnamon, cloves, star anise, sugar and water in a saucepan. Place over a medium–high heat, stirring, for 6–8 minutes, or until the sugar has dissolved. Increase the heat to high until the mixture comes to the boil, then reduce the heat to medium and simmer for 4–5 minutes, stirring occasionally.

2. Transfer the mixture to a blender, add the orange juice, then whizz until puréed. Allow to cool completely.

3. Pour the mixture into 8 x 50 ml/2 fl oz ice pop moulds. Insert the cinnamon sticks (see page 8) and freeze for 5 hours, or until firm.

4. To unmould the ice pops, dip the frozen moulds into warm water for a few seconds and gently release the pops while holding the cinnamon sticks.

Coconut Passion Pops

Makes: 8 ice pops

Prep: 15 minutes

Cool: 1 hour

Freeze: 5–7 hours

Eat: within 3 months
of freezing

The tropical flavours of pineapple, passion fruit and coconut make them natural partners in these refreshing and creamy ice pops.

* juice and pulp of 5 large passion fruit (approximately 150 ml/5 fl oz)
* 250 ml/9 fl oz sugar syrup (see page 6)
* 100 g/3½ oz pineapple flesh, chopped
* 175 ml/6 fl oz coconut cream
* 150 ml/5 fl oz double cream

1. Put the passion fruit juice and pulp in a small saucepan with half the sugar syrup. Place over a medium–high heat, stirring, until the mixture comes to the boil. Remove from the heat, cover and allow to cool completely; this will take about 1 hour.

2. Pour the mixture into 8 x 100 ml/3½ fl oz ice pop moulds and freeze for 2–3 hours, or until firm.

3. When the passion fruit mixture is frozen, put the pineapple, coconut cream, double cream and remaining sugar syrup in a blender and whizz until fairly smooth. Pour over the frozen passion fruit mixture. Insert the ice pop sticks (see page 8) and freeze for 3–4 hours, or until firm.

4. To unmould the ice pops, dip the frozen moulds into warm water for a few seconds and gently release the pops while holding the sticks.

Milky Chai Pops

Makes: 8 ice pops

Prep: 15 minutes

Steep and cool:
2½ hours

Freeze: 5–6 hours

Eat: within 3 months
of freezing

Full of spicy, Eastern flavours, this popular drink makes a great iced dessert and is sure to quickly become a household favourite.

* 200 ml/7 fl oz milk
* 1 star anise
* 10 cloves
* 3 cinnamon sticks
* 10 white peppercorns
* 6 cardamom pods, lightly crushed
* 300 ml/10 fl oz water
* 2 tbsp black tea leaves (Ceylon or English breakfast)
* 100 ml/3½ fl oz sweetened condensed milk

1. Put the milk, star anise, cloves, cinnamon, white peppercorns, cardamom pods and water in a saucepan. Place over a medium–high heat and bring to the boil, stirring. Remove from the heat and allow to steep for 40–50 minutes, to infuse the flavours of the spices.

2. Return the pan to the heat and bring to the boil, stirring. Add the tea leaves, remove from the heat, stir well and allow to steep for 10–15 minutes.

3. Pour through a fine metal sieve into a large jug and discard the tea and spices. Stir in the condensed milk and leave to cool completely.

4. Pour the mixture into 8 x 100 ml/3½ fl oz ice pop moulds. Insert the ice pop sticks (see page 8) and freeze for 5–6 hours, or until firm.

5. To unmould the ice pops, dip the frozen moulds into warm water for a few seconds and gently release the pops while holding the sticks.

Cappuccino Pops

Makes: 8 ice pops

Prep: 15 minutes

Cool: 30 minutes

Freeze: 6–7 hours

Eat: within 3 months of freezing

Coffee made from freshly ground beans is a superb flavouring for any iced dessert. Instant coffee works too, but the flavour will be less intense.

* 150 ml/5 fl oz sweetened condensed milk
* 100 ml/3½ fl oz double cream
* 600 ml/1 pint brewed espresso coffee, at room temperature
* 1 tbsp cocoa powder

1. Put 50 ml/2 fl oz of the condensed milk into a measuring jug with the double cream and lightly whisk until well combined and slightly thickened.

2. Pour the mixture into 8 x 100 ml/3½ fl oz ice pop moulds and freeze for 2 hours, or until firm.

3. Meanwhile, whisk the remaining condensed milk with the coffee and cocoa powder in a bowl until well blended. Leave to cool completely.

4. Pour this mixture over the frozen cream mixture. Insert the ice pop sticks (see page 8) and freeze for 4–5 hours, or until firm.

5. To unmould the ice pops, dip the frozen moulds into warm water for a few seconds and gently release the pops while holding the sticks.

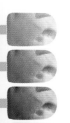

Pops with a Kick

Strawberry Margarita Pops   64

Peach Bellini Pops   66

Apple Martini Lollies   68

Mojito Pops   70

Pina Colada Lollies   72

Gin and Tonic Lollies   74

Cosmopolitan Pops   76

Black Russian Pops   78

Strawberry Margarita Pops

Makes: 8 ice pops

Prep: 10 minutes

Freeze: 6–8 hours

Eat: within 3 months of freezing

Seriously fruity, but with a light boozy kick, these pops add a Mexican flamboyance to any party.

* 500 g/1 lb 2 oz strawberries, hulled and chopped
* 100 ml/3½ fl oz sugar syrup (see page 6)
* juice and finely grated rind of 1 lime
* 2 tbsp tequila
* 1 tbsp cointreau
* a pinch of salt
* 150 ml/5 fl oz water
* 25 g/1 oz caster sugar, to serve

1. Put all the ingredients except the caster sugar in a blender and whizz until smooth.

2. Pour the mixture into 8 x 80 ml/2½ fl oz ice pop moulds. Insert the ice pop sticks (see page 8) and freeze for 6–8 hours, or until firm.

3. To unmould the ice pops, dip the frozen moulds into warm water for a few seconds and gently release the pops while holding the sticks.

4. To serve the ice pops, tip the caster sugar on to a plate and dip the ice pops in the sugar.

Peach Bellini Pops

Makes: 8 ice pops
Prep: 15 minutes
Freeze: 8–10 hours
Eat: within 3 months
of freezing

The ultimate Italian summer flavour experience, these
heady iced treats will have your guests coming back
for more.

* 2 ripe peaches, peeled, stoned
  and cut into small dice
* 2 tbsp peach liqueur
* 300 ml/10 fl oz prosecco
* 250 ml/9 fl oz sugar syrup
  (see page 6)

1. Divide the peaches between 8 x 60 ml/2¼ fl oz
ice pop moulds or plastic Champagne glasses.

2. Put the peach liqueur, prosecco and sugar
syrup into a measuring jug and stir together well.

3. Pour the mixture into the moulds or plastic
glasses. Insert the ice pop sticks (see page 8) and
freeze for 8–10 hours, or until firm.

4. To unmould the ice pops, wrap the frozen moulds
or plastic glasses in a hot water-soaked tea-towel
for a few seconds and gently release the pops while
holding the sticks.

Apple Martini Lollies

Makes: 8 ice pops

Prep: 10 minutes

Freeze: 8–10 hours

Eat: within 3 months of freezing

These 'cocktails on a stick' are a great summer treat!
Apple and lemon rind give a twist to the classic Martini.

* 400 ml/14 fl oz clear apple juice
* 100 ml/3½ fl oz sugar syrup (see page 6)
* finely grated rind of 1 lemon
* 3 tbsp gin
* 1 tbsp dry vermouth
* 8 very thin slices of a small apple

1. Put all the ingredients except the apple slices into a measuring jug and stir together well.

2. Pour the mixture into 8 x 80 ml/2½ fl oz ice pop moulds or plastic Martini glasses. Drop an apple slice into each mould or plastic glass. Insert the ice pop sticks or plastic cocktail sticks (see page 8) and freeze for 8–10 hours, or until firm.

3. To unmould the ice pops, wrap the frozen moulds or plastic glasses in a hot water-soaked tea-towel for a few seconds and gently release the pops while holding the sticks.

Mojito Pops

Makes: 8 ice pops

Prep: 15 minutes

Freeze: 10–12 hours

Eat: within 3 months
of freezing

Get your Mojito fix in an ice pop. Now you can cool down with one of your favourite drinks and never worry about getting your glass mixed up with someone else's! For a child-friendly version, simply leave out the rum.

* juice of 6 limes
* 600 ml/1 pint chilled soda water
* 50 g/1¾ oz fresh mint leaves
* 3 limes, cut into wedges
* 100 g/3½ oz caster sugar
* 2 tbsp white rum

1. Put the lime juice and soda water into a measuring jug and stir together well.

2. Stir in the mint leaves, lime wedges, sugar and rum. Using a 'muddler' or thick wooden spoon or mallet, mash together all the ingredients until well blended.

3. Pour the mixture into 8 x 100 ml/3½ fl oz ice pop moulds. Divide the lime wedges and mint leaves evenly between them. Insert the ice pop sticks (see page 8) and freeze for 10–12 hours, or until firm.

4. To unmould the ice pops, dip the frozen moulds into warm water for a few seconds and gently release the pops while holding the sticks.

Pina Colada Lollies

Makes: 8 ice pops

Prep: 15 minutes

Freeze: 6–8 hours

Eat: within 3 months of freezing

The cool and refreshing combination of pineapple, coconut and rum will delight grown-up ice pop lovers. A perfect way to beat the summer heat, these are elegant enough to impress and far too delicious to resist.

* 600 g/1 lb 5 oz pineapple flesh, finely diced
* 200 ml/7 fl oz coconut milk
* 6 tbsp caster sugar
* 2 tbsp Malibu

1. Drop a tablespoon of the diced pineapple flesh into each of 8 x 100 ml/3½ fl oz ice pop moulds.

2. Put the remaining pineapple flesh in a blender with the coconut milk, sugar and Malibu and whizz until smooth.

3. Sieve using a fine metal sieve, pressing down to extract all the juice. Discard the solids. Pour the mixture into the ice pop moulds. Insert the ice pop sticks (see page 8) and freeze for 6–8 hours, or until firm.

4. To unmould the ice pops, dip the frozen moulds into warm water for a few seconds and gently release the pops while holding the sticks.

Gin and Tonic Lollies

Makes: 8 ice pops

Prep: 10 minutes

Freeze: 6–8 hours

Eat: within 3 months of freezing

A naughty yet refreshing grown-up ice pop for a hot summer's day – ideal for sharing in the early evening, as the sun goes down.

* 250 ml/9 fl oz sugar syrup (see page 6)
* 2 tbsp gin
* 400 ml/14 fl oz tonic water
* juice of 1 lime
* 16 very thin slices of a small cucumber

1. Put the sugar syrup, gin, tonic water and lime juice into a measuring jug and stir together well.

2. Pour the mixture into 8 x 80 ml/2½ fl oz ice pop moulds. Drop 2 slices of cucumber into each mould. Insert the ice pop sticks (see page 8) and freeze for 6–8 hours, or until firm.

3. To unmould the ice pops, dip the frozen moulds into warm water for a few seconds and gently release the pops while holding the sticks.

 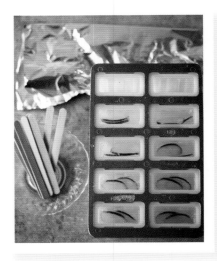

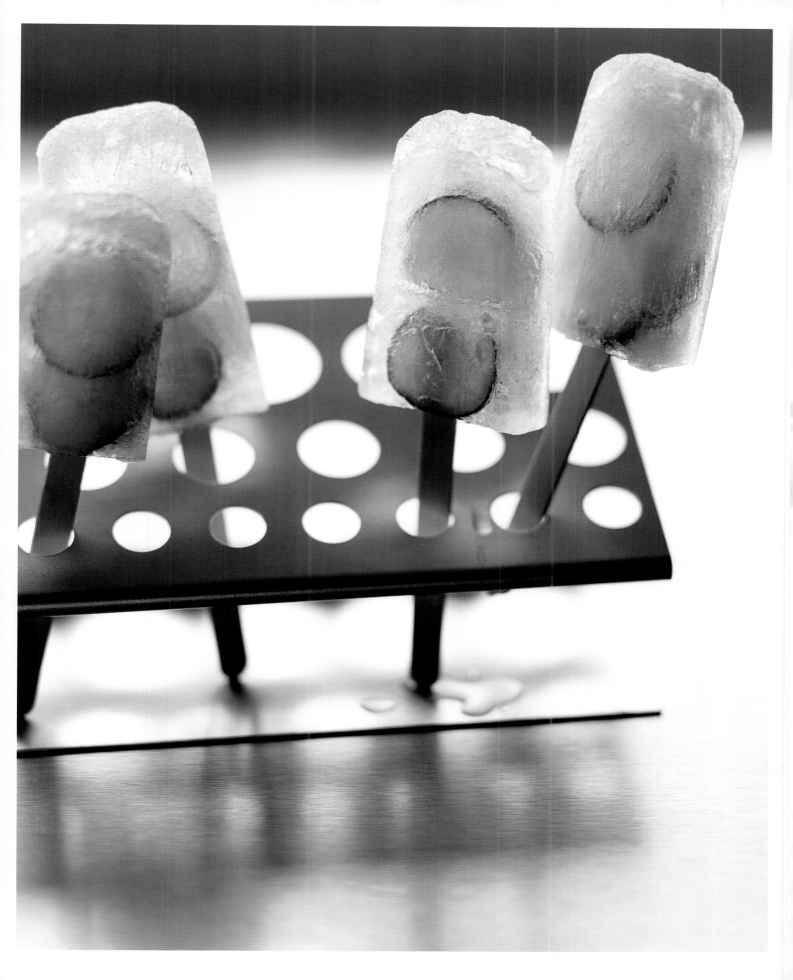

Cosmopolitan Pops

Makes: 8 ice pops

Prep: 10 minutes

Freeze: 8–10 hours

Eat: within 3 months
of freezing

Make these colourful and lightly alcoholic pops to serve
at the end of a long summer lunch. Keep in the freezer
until the last minute, and for impressive entertaining,
serve them on a tray filled with ice cubes or crushed ice.

* 250 ml/9 fl oz sugar syrup
  (see page 6)
* 500 ml/18 fl oz cranberry juice
* 2 tbsp vodka
* 1 tbsp Cointreau
* juice of 1 lime
* finely grated rind of
  1 clementine

1. Put all the ingredients into a measuring jug
and stir well.

2. Pour the mixture into 8 x 100 ml/3½ fl oz ice pop
moulds. Insert the ice pop sticks (see page 8) and
freeze for 8–10 hours, or until firm.

3. To unmould the ice pops, dip the frozen moulds
into warm water for a few seconds and gently
release the pops while holding the sticks.

Black Russian Pops

Makes: 8 ice pops

Prep: 10 minutes

Freeze: 8–10 hours

Eat: within 3 months of freezing; eat within 24 hours if using thick shot glasses

Dark and decadent, these smooth ice pops make a great after-dinner treat on a hot summer's night.

* 1 tbsp Kahlua or Tia Maria
* 500 ml/18 fl oz cola
* 2 tbsp vodka

1. Put all the ingredients into a measuring jug and stir together well.

2. Pour the mixture into 8 x 50 ml/2 fl oz ice pop moulds or thick shot glasses. Insert the ice pop sticks (see page 8) and freeze for 8–10 hours, or until firm.

3. To unmould the ice pops, wrap the frozen moulds or glasses in a hot water-soaked tea-towel for a few seconds and gently release the pops while holding the sticks.

Index

alcohol 8
  Apple Martini Lollies 68
  Black Russian Pops 78
  Chocolate Mint Delights 36
  Cosmopolitan Pops 76
  Gin and Tonic Lollies 74
  Mojito Pops 70
  Peach Bellini Pops 66
  Pina Colada Lollies 72
  Strawberry Margarita Pops 64
apple: Apple Martini Lollies 68

banana
  Banana Split Lollies 42
  Raspberry and Banana Layer Pops 20
basil: Watermelon Chill-out Lollies 52
Black Russian Pops 78
Blackberry and Orange Bursts 26
blackcurrants: Very Cherry Ripple Pops 22
blender 7
Blueberry and Pink Lemonade Lollies 14

cantaloupe melons: Summer Melon
  Medley Pops 16
Cappuccino Pops 60
chai: Milky Chai Pops 58
cherry jam: Very Cherry Ripple Pops 22
chillies: Lime and Chilli Sorbet Lollies 50
chocolate
  Banana Split Lollies 42
  Choc Berry Rockets 32
  Chocolate Mint Delights 36
  Dark Chocolate Ripple Pops 44
  Triple Chocolate Heaven Pops 40
cinnamon
  Milky Chai Pops 58
  Spiced Plum Pops 54
coconut cream/milk
  Banana Split Lollies 42
  Coconut Passion Pops 56
  Pina Colada Lollies 72
coffee: Cappuccino Pops 60
cola 8
  Black Russian Pops 78
condensed milk
  Cappuccino Pops 60
  Milky Chai Pops 58
Cosmopolitan Pops 76
cranberries
  Cosmopolitan Pops 76
  Strawberry Sensations 12

cream
  Cappuccino Pops 60
  Coconut Passion Pops 56
  Dark Chocolate Ripple Pops 44
  Peaches and Cream Pops 30
  Triple Chocolate Heaven Pops 40
cucumber: Gin and Tonic Lollies 74

Dark Chocolate Ripple Pops 44

equipment 7

Fruit Cocktail Pops 18

Gin and Tonic Lollies 74
grapefruit: Pomegranate Power Pops 24

honey
  Honeydew Heaven Pops 48
  Mango Fruity Crush Lollies 34
  Raspberry and Banana Layer Pops 20
honeydew melons: Honeydew Heaven Pops 48
hundreds and thousands: Choc Berry Rockets 32

kiwi fruit: Fruit Cocktail Pops 18

lemon
  Apple Martini Lollies 68
  Choc Berry Rockets 32
  Gin and Tonic Lollies 74
  Very Cherry Ripple Pops 22
lemon grass: Honeydew Heaven Pops 48
lemonade 8
  Blueberry and Pink Lemonade Lollies 14
  Honeydew Heaven Pops 48
lime
  Cosmopolitan Pops 76
  Lime and Chilli Sorbet Lollies 50
  Mojito Pops 70
  Strawberry Margarita Pops 64
  Summer Melon Medley Pops 16
  Watermelon Chill-out Lollies 52
lolly sticks 7, 8
  inserting 8

mango: Mango Fruity Crush Lollies 34
melon
  Honeydew Heaven Pops 48
  Summer Melon Medley Pops 16
  Watermelon Chill-out Lollies 52
milk
  Milky Chai Pops 58
  see also condensed milk
mint
  Chocolate Mint Delights 36
  Mojito Pops 70

moulds 7, 8
  filling 8
  unmolding 8

orange
  Blackberry and Orange Bursts 26
  Spiced Plum Pops 54

passion fruit: Coconut Passion Pops 56
peach
  Fruit Cocktail Pops 18
  Peach Bellini Pops 66
  Peaches and Cream Pops 30
Pina Colada Lollies 72
pineapple
  Coconut Passion Pops 56
  Pina Colada Lollies 72
plum: Spiced Plum Pops 54
pomegranate: Pomegranate Power Pops 24

raspberry
  Choc Berry Rockets 32
  Raspberry and Banana Layer Pops 20
  Yogurt Raspberry Ripple Pops 38

Spiced Plum Pops 54
strawberry
  Fruit Cocktail Pops 18
  Mango Fruity Crush Lollies 34
  Strawberry Margarita Pops 64
  Strawberry Sensations 12
sugar syrup 6
Summer Melon Medley Pops 16

tea: Milky Chai Pops 58
techniques 8
Triple Chocolate Heaven Pops 40

vanilla
  Banana Split Lollies 42
  Mango Fruity Crush Lollies 34
  Peaches and Cream Pops 30
  Raspberry and Banana Layer Pops 20
  Yogurt Raspberry Ripple Pops 38
  Very Cherry Ripple Pops 22

watermelon
  Summer Melon Medley Pops 16
  Watermelon Chill-out Lollies 52

yogurt
  Banana Split Lollies 42
  Mango Fruity Crush Lollies 34
  Raspberry and Banana Layer Pops 20
  Very Cherry Ripple Pops 22
  Yogurt Raspberry Ripple Pops 38